The
UNITED
STATES
PRESIDENTS

James
MADISON

Megan M. Gunderson

Big Buddy Books
An Imprint of Abdo Publishing
abdopublishing.com

abdopublishing.com

Published by Abdo Publishing, a division of ABDO, PO Box 398166, Minneapolis, Minnesota 55439.
Copyright © 2017 by Abdo Consulting Group, Inc. International copyrights reserved in all countries. No
part of this book may be reproduced in any form without written permission from the publisher. Big Buddy
Books™ is a trademark and logo of Abdo Publishing.

Printed in the United States of America, North Mankato, Minnesota
062016
092016

 THIS BOOK CONTAINS
RECYCLED MATERIALS

Design: Sarah DeYoung, Mighty Media, Inc.
Production: Mighty Media, Inc.
Editor: Lauren Kukla
Cover Photograph: Getty Images
Interior Photographs: Alamy (p. 11); AP Images (pp. 9, 15, 21); Corbis (pp. 5, 7, 23); Getty Images (pp. 17,
    25, 29); Library of Congress (pp. 6, 13); National Archives (p. 19); North Wind (pp. 7, 27).

Cataloging-in-Publication Data

Names: Gunderson, Megan M., author.
Title: James Madison / by Megan M. Gunderson.
Description: Minneapolis, MN : Abdo Publishing, [2017] | Series: United States
    presidents | Includes bibliographical references and index.
Identifiers: LCCN 2015957494 | ISBN 9781680781076 (lib. bdg.) |
    ISBN 9781680775273 (ebook)
Subjects: LCSH: Madison, James, 1751-1836--Juvenile literature. | Presidents--
    United States--Biography--Juvenile literature. | United States--Politics and
    government--1809-1817--Juvenile literature.
Classification: DDC 973.5/1092 [B]--dc23
LC record available at http://lccn.loc.gov/2015957494

Contents

James Madison

James Madison was the fourth president of the United States. He was an important **political** leader. He served in the Continental Congress. He also helped write the US **Constitution**. As a congressman, Madison **supported** the **Bill of Rights**.

Madison became president in 1809. President Madison led the nation through the **War of 1812**. He served two terms as president. He remains one of the most important leaders in American history.

Timeline

1751

On March 16, James Madison was born in Port Conway, Virginia.

1780

In March, Madison began serving in the Continental Congress.

1787

Madison attended the **Constitutional** Convention, where he helped plan the US Constitution.

1801

President Thomas Jefferson made Madison **secretary of state**.

6

1812

The **War of 1812** began on June 18. Madison was reelected president.

1809

On March 4, Madison became the fourth US president.

1814

On December 24, the United States and Great Britain signed a **treaty** to end the War of 1812.

1836

On June 28, James Madison died.

Early Life

James Madison was born on March 16, 1751, in Port Conway, Virginia. His parents were James and Eleanor Madison. When James was 11, he went away to school. Then, at 16, James returned home to study.

★ FAST FACTS ★

Born: March 16, 1751

Wife: Dolley Payne Todd (1768–1849)

Children: none

Political Party: Democratic-Republican

Age at Inauguration: 57

Years Served: 1809–1817

Vice Presidents: George Clinton, Elbridge Gerry

Died: June 28, 1836, age 85

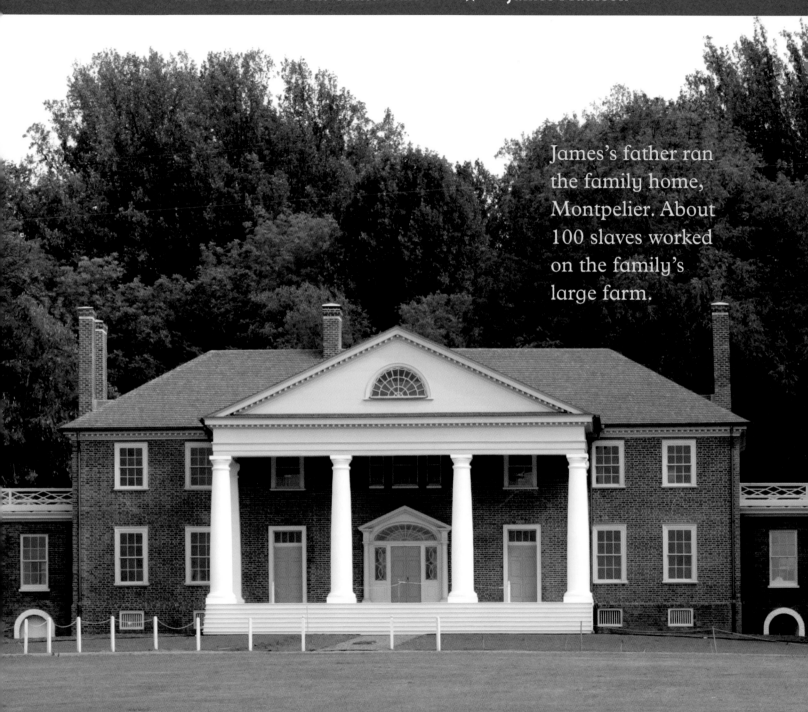

James's father ran the family home, Montpelier. About 100 slaves worked on the family's large farm.

College

In 1769, James was ready for college. He moved to New Jersey. There, he attended the College of New Jersey in Princeton.

At the time, America was ruled by Great Britain. However, many colonists felt British laws were unfair. James agreed. So, he joined an anti-British student club.

James finished school in 1771. But he stayed in Princeton to study for six more months. Then, in 1772, James returned home. There, he studied law, history, and **politics**.

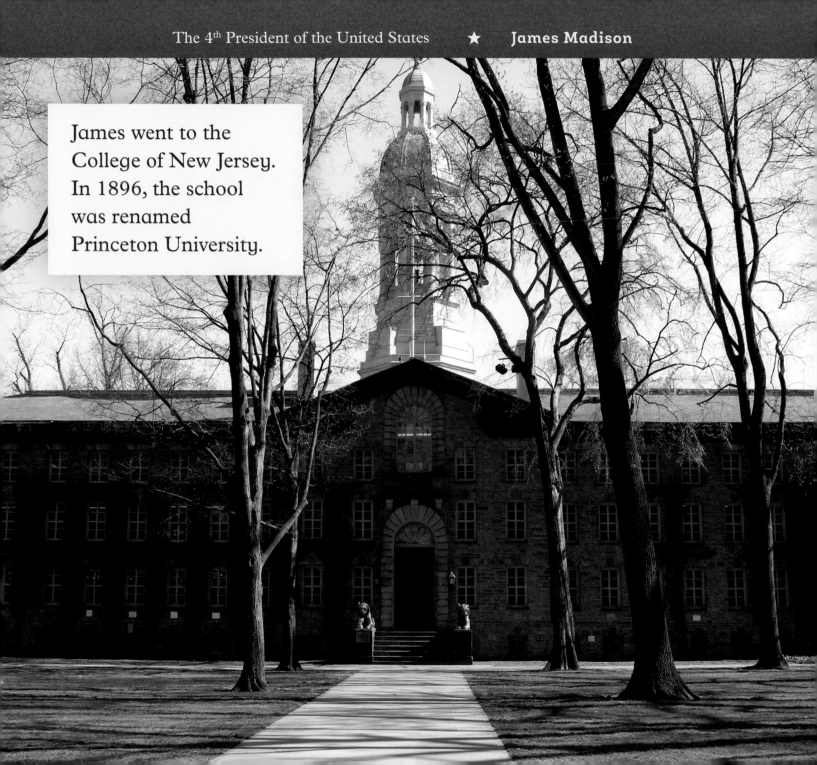

James went to the College of New Jersey. In 1896, the school was renamed Princeton University.

Virginia Leader

In 1774, Madison was elected to his first public office. He earned a position on the Orange County **Committee** of Safety. This group was in charge of the local **militia**. It also provided local government.

The following year, the **American Revolution** began. In May 1776, Madison became a **delegate** to the Virginia Convention. This meeting called for Virginia's independence from Great Britain. Madison helped write Virginia's new **constitution**.

Madison joined the Orange County militia. However, his health was poor, so he did not serve long.

Meanwhile, other colonies also called for independence. On July 4, 1776, the Continental Congress approved the Declaration of Independence. In it, America stated it was independent from Great Britain.

The same year, Madison served in the Virginia **legislature**. There, Madison met Thomas Jefferson. Together, they fought for freedom of religion. They also **supported** free education.

★ DID YOU KNOW? ★

James Madison was the shortest US president. He was just five feet six inches (1.7 m) tall.

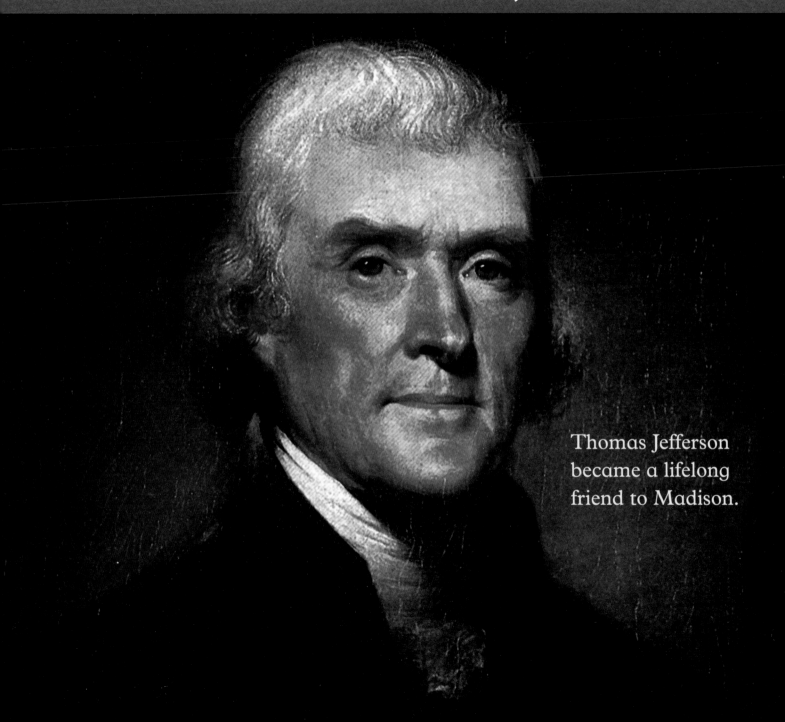

Thomas Jefferson
became a lifelong
friend to Madison.

A New Nation

In 1780, Madison began serving in the Continental Congress. **Delegates** from each state made up this group. It was a temporary government for all the states.

Madison also worked to make the Mississippi River the nation's western border. His plan was accomplished with the **Treaty** of Paris, which was signed in 1783. This treaty also ended the **American Revolution**.

At 29, Madison was the youngest member of the Continental Congress.

US Constitution

In 1787, Madison attended the **Constitutional** Convention. There, he called for a stronger national government. However, the power would be divided between three branches. These are the executive, judicial, and **legislative** branches.

On September 17, Madison and 38 **delegates** signed the US Constitution. Madison and two others then wrote a series of 85 papers. Together, they are called the **Federalist** papers. These papers explained the US Constitution.

The separation of powers would keep the government from being too strong. This became the basic idea behind the US Constitution.

New Government

In 1789, George Washington became the first US president. Madison helped write his **inaugural** speech. He also helped Washington choose the first **cabinet** members.

The same year, Madison began serving in the US House of **Representatives**. In the House, Madison **supported** the **Bill of Rights**. Meanwhile, Madison married Dolley Payne Todd in 1794.

Madison and Dolley
had no children
of their own. But
together, they raised
Dolley's son from
her first marriage.

Secretary of State

John Adams was the second US president. He was a **Federalist**. Madison and Jefferson disagreed with the Federalists about the national government's powers. So, they formed the **Democratic-Republican** Party.

In 1801, Jefferson became the third US president. He made Madison his **secretary of state**. In 1803, Madison **supported** the Louisiana Purchase. With this, the United States gained the land between the Mississippi River and the Rocky Mountains.

Madison was the second secretary of state to later become president.

President Madison

In 1808, Madison ran for president. He beat **Federalist** Charles C. Pinckney. On March 4, 1809, Madison became the fourth US president.

At the time, France and Great Britain were at war. Madison tried to keep the country out of the war. But the British were attacking US ships. So, Madison felt he had no choice but to join the war.

On June 18, 1812, the **War of 1812** began. That same year, Madison faced reelection. He won again!

PRESIDENT MADISON'S CABINET

First Term
March 4, 1809–March 4, 1813

★ **STATE:** Robert Smith,
James Monroe (from 1811)

★ **TREASURY:** Albert Gallatin

★ **WAR:** John Smith,
William Eustis (from April 8, 1809),
John Armstrong (from February 5, 1813)

★ **NAVY:** Robert Smith,
Paul Hamilton (from May 15, 1809),
William Jones (from January 19, 1813)

★ **ATTORNEY GENERAL:** Caesar A. Rodney,
William Pinkney (from January 6, 1812)

Second Term
March 4, 1813–March 4, 1817

★ **STATE:** James Monroe

★ **TREASURY:** Albert Gallatin,
George W. Campbell (from February 9, 1814),
Alexander J. Dallas (from October 14, 1814),
William H. Crawford (from October 22, 1816)

★ **WAR:** John Armstrong,
James Monroe (from October 1, 1814),
William H. Crawford (from August 8, 1815)

★ **NAVY:** William Jones,
Benjamin W. Crowninshield (from January 16, 1815)

★ **ATTORNEY GENERAL:** William Pinkney,
Richard Rush (from February 11, 1814)

25

The **War of 1812** continued in Madison's second term. Finally, on December 24, 1814, the United States and Great Britain signed a **treaty**. Two months later, the war ended.

During the same month, a group of **Federalists** met. The **delegates** came from five New England states. They wanted more independence for their states.

Many people feared the states planned to leave the country. So, the Federalists were seen as **unpatriotic**. As a result, Madison became even more popular.

★ SUPREME COURT APPOINTMENTS ★

Gabriel Duvall: 1811

Joseph Story: 1812

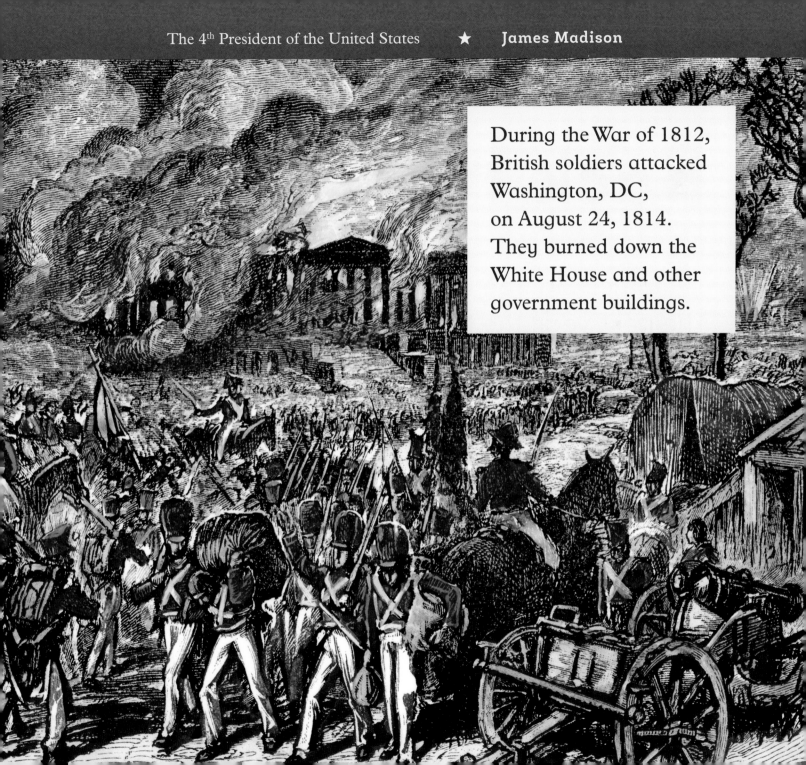

During the War of 1812, British soldiers attacked Washington, DC, on August 24, 1814. They burned down the White House and other government buildings.

Back Home

James Monroe was elected president in 1816. The next year, the Madisons returned to Virginia. Then, in 1829, Madison attended the Virginia **Constitutional** Convention. This was his last public office. On June 28, 1836, James Madison died.

Today, Madison is remembered as the Father of the Constitution. He helped **expand** the nation's borders. He also led the nation through the **War of 1812**. James Madison is one of the most important early leaders in US history.

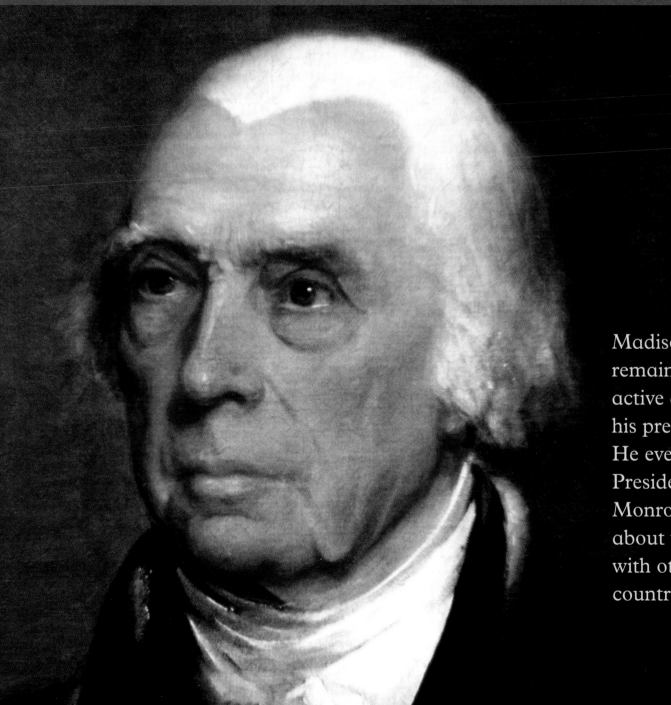

Madison remained active after his presidency. He even gave President Monroe advice about working with other countries.

Office of the President

Branches of Government

The US government has three branches. They are the executive, legislative, and judicial branches. Each branch has some power over the others. This is called a system of checks and balances.

★ Executive Branch

The executive branch enforces laws. It is made up of the president, the vice president, and the president's cabinet. The president represents the United States around the world. He or she also signs bills into law and leads the military.

★ Legislative Branch

The legislative branch makes laws, maintains the military, and regulates trade. It also has the power to declare war. This branch includes the Senate and the House of Representatives. Together, these two houses form Congress.

★ Judicial Branch

The judicial branch interprets laws. It is made up of district courts, courts of appeals, and the Supreme Court. District courts try cases. Sometimes people disagree with a trial's outcome. Then he or she may appeal. If a court of appeals supports the ruling, a person may appeal to the Supreme Court.

Qualifications for Office

To be president, a candidate must be at least 35 years old. The person must be a natural-born US citizen. He or she must also have lived in the United States for at least 14 years.

Electoral College

The US presidential election is an indirect election. Voters from each state choose electors. These electors represent their state in the Electoral College. Each elector has one electoral vote. Electors cast their vote for the candidate with the highest number of votes from people in their state. A candidate must receive the majority of Electoral College votes to win.

Term of Office

Each president may be elected to two four-year terms. The presidential election is held on the Tuesday after the first Monday in November. The president is sworn in on January 20 of the following year. At that time, he or she takes the oath of office.
It states:

> I do solemnly swear (or affirm) that I will faithfully execute the office of President of the United States, and will to the best of my ability, preserve, protect and defend the Constitution of the United States.

Line of Succession

The Presidential Succession Act of 1947 states who becomes president if the president cannot serve. The vice president is first in the line. Next are the Speaker of the House and the President Pro Tempore of the Senate. It may happen that none of these individuals is able to serve. Then the office falls to the president's cabinet members. They would take office in the order in which each department was created:

Secretary of State

Secretary of the Treasury

Secretary of Defense

Attorney General

Secretary of the Interior

Secretary of Agriculture

Secretary of Commerce

Secretary of Labor

Secretary of Health and Human Services

Secretary of Housing and Urban Development

Secretary of Transportation

Secretary of Energy

Secretary of Education

Secretary of Veterans Affairs

Secretary of Homeland Security

Benefits

★ While in office, the president receives a salary. It is $400,000 per year. He or she lives in the White House. The president also has 24-hour Secret Service protection.

★ The president may travel on a Boeing 747 jet. This special jet is called Air Force One. It can hold 70 passengers. It has kitchens, a dining room, sleeping areas, and more. Air Force One can fly halfway around the world before needing to refuel. It can even refuel in flight!

★ When the president travels by car, he or she uses Cadillac One. It is a Cadillac Deville that has been modified. The car has heavy armor and communications systems. The president may even take Cadillac One along when visiting other countries.

★ The president also travels on a helicopter. It is called Marine One. It may also be taken along when the president visits other countries.

★ Sometimes the president needs to get away with family and friends. Camp David is the official presidential retreat. It is located in Maryland. The US Navy maintains the retreat. The US Marine Corps keeps it secure. The camp offers swimming, tennis, golf, and hiking.

★ When the president leaves office, he or she receives lifetime Secret Service protection. He or she also receives a yearly pension of $203,700. The former president also receives money for office space, supplies, and staff.

PRESIDENTS AND THEIR TERMS

PRESIDENT	PARTY	TOOK OFFICE	LEFT OFFICE	TERMS SERVED	VICE PRESIDENT
George Washington	None	April 30, 1789	March 4, 1797	Two	John Adams
John Adams	Federalist	March 4, 1797	March 4, 1801	One	Thomas Jefferson
Thomas Jefferson	Democratic-Republican	March 4, 1801	March 4, 1809	Two	Aaron Burr, George Clinton
James Madison	Democratic-Republican	March 4, 1809	March 4, 1817	Two	George Clinton, Elbridge Gerry
James Monroe	Democratic-Republican	March 4, 1817	March 4, 1825	Two	Daniel D. Tompkins
John Quincy Adams	Democratic-Republican	March 4, 1825	March 4, 1829	One	John C. Calhoun
Andrew Jackson	Democrat	March 4, 1829	March 4, 1837	Two	John C. Calhoun, Martin Van Buren
Martin Van Buren	Democrat	March 4, 1837	March 4, 1841	One	Richard M. Johnson
William H. Harrison	Whig	March 4, 1841	April 4, 1841	Died During First Term	John Tyler
John Tyler	Whig	April 6, 1841	March 4, 1845	Completed Harrison's Term	Office Vacant
James K. Polk	Democrat	March 4, 1845	March 4, 1849	One	George M. Dallas
Zachary Taylor	Whig	March 5, 1849	July 9, 1850	Died During First Term	Millard Fillmore

PRESIDENT	PARTY	TOOK OFFICE	LEFT OFFICE	TERMS SERVED	VICE PRESIDENT
Millard Fillmore	Whig	July 10, 1850	March 4, 1853	Completed Taylor's Term	Office Vacant
Franklin Pierce	Democrat	March 4, 1853	March 4, 1857	One	William R.D. King
James Buchanan	Democrat	March 4, 1857	March 4, 1861	One	John C. Breckinridge
Abraham Lincoln	Republican	March 4, 1861	April 15, 1865	Served One Term, Died During Second Term	Hannibal Hamlin, Andrew Johnson
Andrew Johnson	Democrat	April 15, 1865	March 4, 1869	Completed Lincoln's Second Term	Office Vacant
Ulysses S. Grant	Republican	March 4, 1869	March 4, 1877	Two	Schuyler Colfax, Henry Wilson
Rutherford B. Hayes	Republican	March 3, 1877	March 4, 1881	One	William A. Wheeler
James A. Garfield	Republican	March 4, 1881	September 19, 1881	Died During First Term	Chester Arthur
Chester Arthur	Republican	September 20, 1881	March 4, 1885	Completed Garfield's Term	Office Vacant
Grover Cleveland	Democrat	March 4, 1885	March 4, 1889	One	Thomas A. Hendricks
Benjamin Harrison	Republican	March 4, 1889	March 4, 1893	One	Levi P. Morton
Grover Cleveland	Democrat	March 4, 1893	March 4, 1897	One	Adlai E. Stevenson
William McKinley	Republican	March 4, 1897	September 14, 1901	Served One Term, Died During Second Term	Garret A. Hobart, Theodore Roosevelt

PRESIDENT	PARTY	TOOK OFFICE	LEFT OFFICE	TERMS SERVED	VICE PRESIDENT
Theodore Roosevelt	Republican	September 14, 1901	March 4, 1909	Completed McKinley's Second Term, Served One Term	Office Vacant, Charles Fairbanks
William Taft	Republican	March 4, 1909	March 4, 1913	One	James S. Sherman
Woodrow Wilson	Democrat	March 4, 1913	March 4, 1921	Two	Thomas R. Marshall
Warren G. Harding	Republican	March 4, 1921	August 2, 1923	Died During First Term	Calvin Coolidge
Calvin Coolidge	Republican	August 3, 1923	March 4, 1929	Completed Harding's Term, Served One Term	Office Vacant, Charles Dawes
Herbert Hoover	Republican	March 4, 1929	March 4, 1933	One	Charles Curtis
Franklin D. Roosevelt	Democrat	March 4, 1933	April 12, 1945	Served Three Terms, Died During Fourth Term	John Nance Garner, Henry A. Wallace, Harry S. Truman
Harry S. Truman	Democrat	April 12, 1945	January 20, 1953	Completed Roosevelt's Fourth Term, Served One Term	Office Vacant, Alben Barkley
Dwight D. Eisenhower	Republican	January 20, 1953	January 20, 1961	Two	Richard Nixon
John F. Kennedy	Democrat	January 20, 1961	November 22, 1963	Died During First Term	Lyndon B. Johnson
Lyndon B. Johnson	Democrat	November 22, 1963	January 20, 1969	Completed Kennedy's Term, Served One Term	Office Vacant, Hubert H. Humphrey
Richard Nixon	Republican	January 20, 1969	August 9, 1974	Completed First Term, Resigned During Second Term	Spiro T. Agnew, Gerald Ford

PRESIDENT	PARTY	TOOK OFFICE	LEFT OFFICE	TERMS SERVED	VICE PRESIDENT
Gerald Ford	Republican	August 9, 1974	January 20, 1977	Completed Nixon's Second Term	Nelson A. Rockefeller
Jimmy Carter	Democrat	January 20, 1977	January 20, 1981	One	Walter Mondale
Ronald Reagan	Republican	January 20, 1981	January 20, 1989	Two	George H.W. Bush
George H.W. Bush	Republican	January 20, 1989	January 20, 1993	One	Dan Quayle
Bill Clinton	Democrat	January 20, 1993	January 20, 2001	Two	Al Gore
George W. Bush	Republican	January 20, 2001	January 20, 2009	Two	Dick Cheney
Barack Obama	Democrat	January 20, 2009	January 20, 2017	Two	Joe Biden

"Our country abounds in the necessaries, the arts, and the comforts of life." James Madison

★ WRITE TO THE PRESIDENT ★

You may write to the president at:
The White House
1600 Pennsylvania Avenue NW
Washington, DC 20500

You may e-mail the president at:
comments@whitehouse.gov

37

Glossary

American Revolution—the war between Americans and the British from 1775 to 1783. The Americans won their freedom from the British.

Bill of Rights—the first ten amendments, or changes, to the US Constitution.

cabinet—a group of advisers chosen by the president to lead government departments.

committee—a group of people selected to make decisions about something.

constitution (kahnt-stuh-TOO-shuhn)—the basic laws that govern a country or a state. Something relating to or following a constitution is constitutional.

delegate—someone who represents other people at a meeting or in a lawmaking group.

Democratic-Republican—a member of the Democratic-Republican political party.

expand—to make larger.

Federalist—a member of the Federalist political party.

inaugurate—to swear into a political office.

legislature—a group of people with the power to make or change laws.

militia (muh-LIH-shuh)—people who help the army in times of need, they are not soldiers.

politics—the art or science of government. Something referring to politics is political. A person who is active in politics is a politician.

representative—someone chosen in an election to act or speak for the people who voted for him or her.

secretary of state—a member of the president's cabinet who handles relations with other countries.

support—to believe in or be in favor of something.

treaty—an agreement made between two or more groups.

unpatriotic—unsupportive of one's country.

War of 1812—a war between the United States and England from 1812 to 1815.

★ WEBSITES ★

To learn more about the US Presidents, visit **booklinks.abdopublishing.com**. These links are routinely monitored and updated to provide the most current information available.

Index